Cambridge **Discovery Education**™
▶ **INTERACTIVE READERS**

Series editor: Bob Hastings

STEALING

David Maule

CAMBRIDGE UNIVERSITY PRESS
Cambridge, New York, Melbourne, Madrid, Cape Town,
Singapore, São Paulo, Delhi, Mexico City

Cambridge University Press
32 Avenue of the Americas, New York, NY 10013-2473, USA

www.cambridge.org
Information on this title: www.cambridge.org/9781107677746

© Cambridge University Press 2014

This publication is in copyright. Subject to statutory exception and to the provisions of relevant collective licensing agreements, no reproduction of any part may take place without the written permission of Cambridge University Press.

First published 2014

Printed in Hong Kong, China, by Golden Cup Printing Company Limited

A catalog record for this publication is available from the British Library.

Library of Congress Cataloging-in-Publication Data

Maule, David.
  Stealing / David Maule.
    pages cm. -- (Cambridge discovery interactive readers)
  ISBN 978-1-107-67774-6 (pbk. : alk. paper)
  1. Stealing--Juvenile literature. 2. English language--Textbooks for foreign speakers. 3. Readers (Elementary) I. Title.

HQ784.S65M38 2013
364.16'2--dc23

                    2013025115

ISBN 978-1-107-67774-6

Additional resources for this publication at www.cambridge.org

Cambridge University Press has no responsibility for the persistence or accuracy of URLs for external or third-party Internet Web sites referred to in this publication and does not guarantee that any content on such Web sites is, or will remain, accurate or appropriate.

Layout services, art direction, book design, and photo research: Q2ABillSMITH GROUP
Editorial services: Hyphen S.A.
Audio production: CityVox, New York
Video production: Q2ABillSMITH GROUP

Contents

Before You Read: Get Ready! 4

CHAPTER 1
Something for Nothing 6

CHAPTER 2
Thieves We Like 8

CHAPTER 3
Heist 12

CHAPTER 4
Stealing from You 16

CHAPTER 5
What Do You Think? 20

After You Read 22

Answer Key 24

Glossary

Before You Read: Get Ready!

Why do people steal – take money or things that aren't theirs? Some people take little things, and others steal lots of money or expensive things. Some of these people are even famous.

Words to Know

Look at the pictures. Then complete the stories below with the correct words.

arrest

diamonds

police

prison

shoplift

In 2005, some men stole $118,000,000 in ❶ _____ from Schiphol Airport in Amsterdam. Later, the ❷ _____ caught some of the men and sent them to ❸ _____.

Winona Ryder is a famous movie star, but in 2001 the police had to ❹ _____ her. Why? Because people saw her ❺ _____ clothes from a store.

Words to Know

Read the paragraph. Then complete the sentences below with the correct highlighted words.

Why do we like to watch movies about pirates? Isn't a pirate a thief on a ship, and nothing more? Well, sometimes it isn't so easy to say what is a crime and what isn't. English kings and queens often gave letters to pirates. These letters said the pirates could take money from Spanish or French ships, and could kill the men on those ships. So who were the criminals? The pirates or the kings and queens?

1. Is it a _____ to steal bread if you're hungry?
2. One of England's most famous _____, Henry VIII, had six wives.
3. Cats _____ birds.
4. Many _____ lived in the Caribbean in the 1600s.
5. A car _____ steals cars.
6. Some _____ today use the Internet to steal from people.

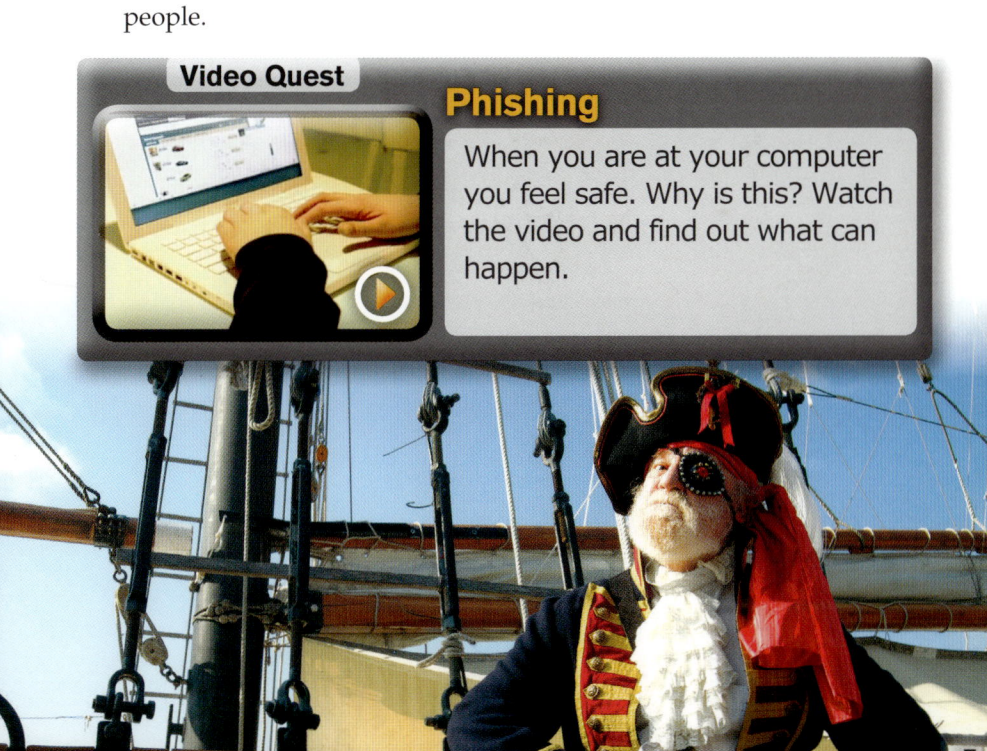

Video Quest

Phishing

When you are at your computer you feel safe. Why is this? Watch the video and find out what can happen.

CHAPTER 1

Something for Nothing

DO YOU ALWAYS DO THE RIGHT THING?

A one hundred dollar bill

How **honest** are you? Answer these questions to find out! Read each question, and choose A (10 points) or B (5 points).

1. You pay for some things at the store with a $20 bill. But you don't get back a $10 bill – you get a $100 bill. What do you do?
   - Ⓐ Give it back.
   - Ⓑ Take it and leave.

2. Your friend has a new bike, but you think he stole it. He says you can buy it for $20. What do you do?
   - Ⓐ Say no.
   - Ⓑ Buy it.

3 You find a wallet in the street. There is a lot of money in it. What do you do?
- (A) Take it to the police.
- (B) Take the money – this person has a lot of it.

4 It's a hot day and you really want a drink. You go into a store. The bottle of water costs 80 cents, but you only have 50 cents. What do you do?
- (A) Leave it.
- (B) Steal it – it's only a bottle of water.

Your Points

How many points did you get?

35–40: You are very honest.
25–30: You should try to be more honest.
20: Are the police looking for you?

EVALUATE
Why is it important for people to be honest?

A wallet

Jack cuts down the beanstalk as the giant comes down.

CHAPTER 2

Thieves We Like

WE TELL STORIES ABOUT THIEVES TO CHILDREN. DO THESE STORIES TEACH CHILDREN RIGHT FROM WRONG?

Here is a popular story that parents tell children . . .

Jack lives in a house with his mother. They have no money. They only have a cow. One day the cow gives no more milk. Jack and his mother must sell the cow for money.

On the road to the town, Jack meets a man. "I'll give you five magic[1] beans for the cow," he says. Jack gives him the cow and takes the beans home.

[1] **magic:** When something is magic, it can do things that are usually impossible.

Beans grow on a beanstalk.

Jack's mother is very angry with him. She throws the beans out the window and doesn't give him any dinner.

In the night, the beans grow[2] into a very tall beanstalk, so tall it goes into the clouds. The next day Jack sees the beanstalk and goes up.

Jack comes to a really big house in the sky. It's the home of a giant. He goes inside and the giant's wife gives him food.

Before he leaves, Jack steals money and other things from the house. The giant runs after him. Jack goes down the beanstalk and the giant starts to go down also. When Jack gets to the bottom, he cuts down the beanstalk. The giant falls and dies.

So, is Jack a good boy for getting money for his family, or is he a **thief**? Or, is he both?

[2] **grow:** get bigger

ANALYZE

Think of a favorite story from when you were a child, one about stealing. Did the thief come to a good or bad end? Why?

Jesse James

Ned Kelly

Jack and the Beanstalk is only a story for children. But some people really stole things and killed other people, and we love their stories, too. We make them famous in books and movies.

Jesse James was a poor farmer from Missouri, USA. Jesse and his friends started to steal money from banks and trains. They killed people, too. But people loved reading about them in newspapers.

Ned Kelly also came from a farm, but in Australia. One day, the police put his mother in **prison**, so Ned and his friends killed three policemen. He later stole money from banks and became very famous. People were with Kelly, not with the police.

Pirates are also thieves we like. Stories of pirates from long ago are very popular, especially in the movies. But movie pirates are not like real pirates. Take Henry Morgan (1635–1688), for example.

Morgan, a Welshman, was not poor. He was very rich. He killed many people and stole a lot of money from ships. He also took money from Spanish cities in the Caribbean.

In 1671, Morgan and his men took a lot of the money from Panama City. The Spanish wanted the English king, Charles II, to arrest Morgan. But King Charles liked him and made him *Sir* Henry Morgan.

So **crime** paid Morgan very well.

[3] **actor:** An actor works in the movies.

Video Quest

Blackbeard the Pirate

Watch this video about the pirate Blackbeard. Do you think he really was a bad man or maybe a good actor?[3]

CHAPTER 3

Heist

WHEN PEOPLE STEAL SOMETHING BIG IN A NEW OR DIFFERENT WAY, WE CALL IT A HEIST. HERE ARE TWO FAMOUS ONES – BUT BOTH WENT WRONG.

Paris, Sunday, August 20, 1911

The Louvre is a famous art museum in Paris. Vincenzo Peruggia, an Italian, knows it well because he worked there before. On this day he goes to the museum and stays after it closes. He waits until early the next morning. Then, he takes Leonardo da Vinci's famous painting, *Mona Lisa*, from the wall, puts it under his coat, and walks out.

Two years later, Alfredo Geri gets a letter from Peruggia. Geri buys and sells paintings in Florence. Peruggia writes that he wants to sell the *Mona Lisa*.

The French army in Italy

Geri speaks to the police, then he answers the letter. Peruggia brings the painting to Florence. Geri meets him, but the police also come, and they arrest Peruggia.

Peruggia wasn't just a criminal after easy money. He had a good **reason** to steal the *Mona Lisa*. In the early 1800s, the French army was in Florence, Italy. Peruggia thought that they stole the painting and took it back to France. But this isn't true.

At the end of his life, da Vinci lived in France and finished the painting there. The French king, Frances I, bought it after da Vinci died. But in 1913, many Italians thought the painting's home was in Italy.

EVALUATE
Many works of art in museums come from other countries. Do you think this makes it OK for someone to steal them and take them back to their country?

The Millennium Dome

London, Tuesday, November 7, 2000

De Beers is the biggest diamond business in the world. In 2000, some of their best diamonds were in the Millennium Dome in London. One of these was the famous Millennium Star diamond. Others were very expensive blue diamonds.

Many people came to see them. But some men wanted to steal the diamonds. The Dome is beside the River Thames, so the criminals got a fast boat. It waited for them near the Dome.

14

A digger

The thieves came into the Dome quickly. They drove right through the door in a digger. But the police were waiting for them!

Before the **crime**, one of the criminals talked about it. The story got back to the police. On the day, some police dressed like workers, and others watched the thieves' boat. There were no diamonds in the Dome, only glass copies.[4]

The police arrested all of the thieves. One of the biggest **heists** in history went very wrong.

[4] **copy:** something that looks the same as something else

CHAPTER 4

Stealing from You

YOU MAY LIKE TO READ ABOUT FAMOUS HEISTS AND WATCH MOVIES ABOUT THEM, BUT IT'S DIFFERENT WHEN PEOPLE STEAL FROM YOU. THAT ISN'T SO MUCH FUN.

One day you read this in the newspaper:

> Put your money into Doffma LLC and we'll pay you 1% every month!

So you give them $500, and they pay you $5 a month. It's more than you can get from the bank. Other people put their money into Doffma, and they get money every month, too.

But one day it all stops, and you can't get your money back. You call Doffma LLC, but there's nobody there!

This is called a scam, and it's very old, maybe hundreds of years old. But now, with the Internet, there are new scams, and the scammers come right into your home.

You get this email:

> Dear Susi,
>
> How are you?
>
> I'm in Malaysia on vacation, but last night somebody stole my money, phone, and plane ticket. I can't pay for my hotel, and I can't get home.
>
> Please send me $3,000. I will pay you back very soon.
>
> Your friend,
>
> Jessica

Jessica is a good friend, so you send her the money.

 ANALYZE

Many people send money to Internet scammers. What can we do to stop the scammers stealing from people?

The next day you see Jessica in the street.

"Hi," you say. "Did you get back from Malaysia OK?"

But Jessica was never in Malaysia. What's going on?

Well, people got into your friend's email and sent the same message to all of her contacts.⁵ They scammed you.

⁵**contacts:** the people in your phone and email

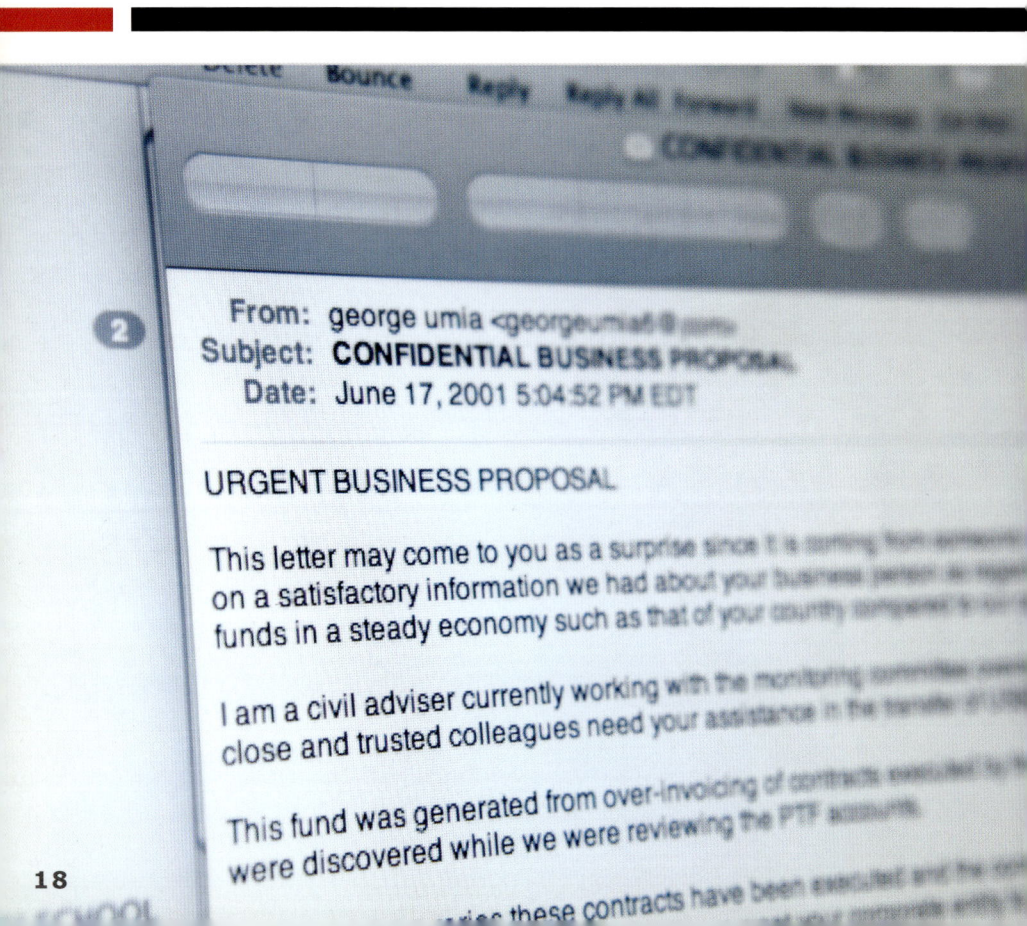

Maybe you're too smart for this. You don't send money to scammers. But if only one person in a hundred sends money, the scammer gets rich.

Today, there are many ways for thieves to steal from you on the Internet. For example, they send you this email:

> From: First Bank of Springfield
> To: Joe
> Re: Your bank account
>
> Dear Joe,
>
> You have some money in our bank, and we need to check your bank account numbers. Please send us your numbers now!

Some people send their numbers, and they lose their money. We call this **identity theft**.

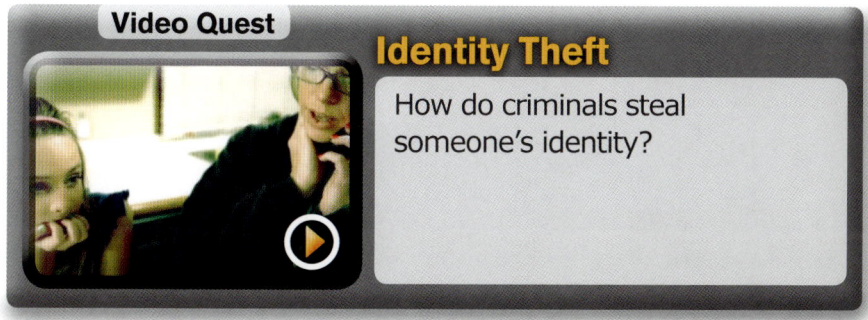

Video Quest

Identity Theft

How do criminals steal someone's identity?

Lindsey Lohan stole this necklace.

CHAPTER 5

What Do You Think?

WHEN IS STEALING NOT REALLY STEALING?

Sometimes famous people **shoplift**. In 2011, singer and actor Lindsey Lohan stole a necklace. She went to prison, but only for five hours – because it was overcrowded.[6] In 2001, Winona Ryder stole clothes worth $5,500, but she didn't go to prison at all.

When famous people shoplift things, they don't usually go to prison. Do you think it's right?

A lot of people steal things from hotels like the Waldorf Astoria – a famous old hotel in New York City. They take things like spoons, cups, and plates.

[6]**overcrowded:** having too many people

Imagine you're having coffee at the Waldorf Astoria. The spoon has the hotel's name on it. You want to take it home with you. You know it's stealing, but the hotel has a lot of spoons. Do you take the spoon?

In this book there are many stories about stealing. But most people don't steal. Why is that? Is it because they're honest? Or is it because they think the police will catch them?

Do you like watching movies and TV shows about heists and other crimes? Do you like to read about criminals? Why?

What about stories for children? Is it OK to tell children stories about stealing? Do you tell them it's OK to steal when you have a good reason? What is a good reason?

Now think about real life. Is it ever OK to steal? When is stealing not really stealing?

The Waldorf Astoria

After You Read

Where From?

Here are some people you met in this book. Which countries did they come from? Write one country on each line.

| Australia | England | France | Italy | United States | Wales |

1. Henry Morgan _____
2. Jesse James _____
3. Charles II _____
4. Francis I _____
5. Ned Kelly _____
6. Vincenzo Peruggia _____

True or False?

Choose True or False for each sentence.

1. Jack stole from the giant.   True   False
2. Ned Kelly stole money but never killed anyone.   True   False
3. Henry Morgan was a poor Englishman.   True   False
4. The French army stole the *Mona Lisa* from Italy.   True   False
5. Thieves stole the Millenium Star diamond in 2000.   True   False
6. There weren't any scams before the Internet.   True   False
7. Winona Ryder went to prison.   True   False
8. The Waldorf Astoria is a prison in New York City.   True   False

Connections

Choose the right word from the box for each connection.

diamonds	farm	king	money

1. Jack stole it from the giant, and Morgan stole it from Panama.   _____
2. Thieves stole these from Schiphol Airport and tried to steal them from the Millennium Dome.   _____
3. Jesse James' family lived on one and so did Ned Kelly's.   _____
4. Charles, Francis, and Henry all had this job.   _____

Complete the Story

Use the words in the box to complete the story.

arrest	criminal	honest	police	prison	shoplifted	thief

Stanley was an ❶ _____ boy, but one day in a store a ❷ _____ put an expensive phone in Stanley's bag. Stanley didn't know about it. When he left the store, they stopped him. They said Stanley ❸ _____ the phone.

The people from the store wanted to call the ❹ _____. Stanley was afraid. Were they going to ❺ _____ him? He didn't want to go to ❻ _____. Then Stanley thought of something.

Stanley and the people from the store watched the video from the store's camera and saw everything. They caught the real ❼ _____, and thanked Stanley. Stanley was very happy to leave that store!

Answer Key

Words to Know, page 4
① diamonds ② police ③ prison ④ arrest ⑤ shoplift

Words to Know, page 5
① crime ② kings ③ kill ④ pirates ⑤ thief ⑥ criminals

Video Quest, page 5
You feel safe because you're at home.

Evaluate, page 7 *Answers will vary.*

Analyze, page 9 *Answers will vary.*

Video Quest, page 11 *Answers will vary.*

Evaluate, page 13 *Answers will vary.*

Analyze, page 17 *Answers will vary.*

Video Quest, page 19
With a little bit of information about you, like your driver's license number or cell phone number, thieves can pretend to be you and open up credit cards and bank accounts.

Where From?, page 22
① Wales ② United States ③ England ④ France
⑤ Australia ⑥ Italy

True or False?, page 22
① True ② False ③ False ④ False ⑤ False ⑥ False
⑦ False ⑧ False

Connections, page 23
① money ② diamonds ③ farm ④ king

Complete the Story, page 23
① honest ② thief / criminal ③ shoplifted ④ police
⑤ arrest ⑥ prison ⑦ criminal / thief